Dolphins

by Leighton Taylor
photographs by Norbert Wu

Lerner Publications Company • Minneapolis, Minnesota

To Davy, Chris, and every child who says hooray for dolphins
—*LT*

To the Day family, the best of friends
—*NW*

Thanks to our series consultant, Sharyn Fenwick, elementary science/math specialist. Mrs. Fenwick was the winner of the National Science Teachers Association 1991 Distinguished Teaching Award. She also was the recipient of the Presidential Award for Excellence in Math and Science Teaching, representing the state of Minnesota at the elementary level in 1992.

Additional photographs are reproduced with permission from: © Thomas Johnson/Earth Views, p. 16; © Bob Cranston, p. 16 (inset); © J. McDonald/Bruce Coleman, Inc., p. 27; Mo Yung Productions: (© Peter Howorth) pp. 33, 36, (© James Watt) p. 34; © William Boyce Photography, p. 40; © Jim Steinberg, The National Audubon Society Collection/Photo Researchers, p. 41.

Early Bird Nature Books were conceptualized by Ruth Berman and designed by Steve Foley. Series editor is Joelle Goldman.

Lerner Publications Company
A division of Lerner Publishing Group
241 First Avenue North
Minneapolis, MN 55401 U.S.A.

Website address: www.lernerbooks.com

Library of Congress Cataloging-in-Publication Data

Taylor, L. R. (Leighton R.)
    Dolphins / by Leighton Taylor ; photographs by Norbert Wu.
      p. cm. — (Early bird nature books)
    Includes index.
    Summary: Introduces the physical characteristics, behavior, habitat, and life cycle of the dolphin.
    ISBN 0-8225-3033-3 (lib. bdg. : alk. paper)
    1. Delphinidae—Juvenile literature. [1. Dolphins.] I. Wu, Norbert, ill. II. Title. III. Series.
QL737.C432T29 1999
599.53—dc21   98–34635

Manufactured in the United States of America
2 3 4 5 6 7 – SP – 08 07 06 05 04 03

Contents

Be a Word Detective

Can you find these words as you read about the dolphin's life? Be a detective and try to figure out what they mean. You can turn to the glossary on page 46 for help.

blowhole

calf

echoes

echolocation

mammals

melon

nursing

predators

prey

schools

streamlined

Chapter 1

These dolphins are bottlenose dolphins. How many kinds of dolphins are there?

What Is a Dolphin?

Do you like dolphins? Most people do. Dolphins are sleek and fast. They race in front of boats. They jump into the air. They seem to be playing as they swim along.

The world has 32 species, or kinds, of dolphins. The species people see most is the bottlenose dolphin. Many zoos keep bottlenose dolphins. Another species is the spinner dolphin. It is nicknamed the "hooray" dolphin. It jumps so high that people want to shout, "Hooray!"

Spinner dolphins often spin when they jump.

A killer whale is a kind of dolphin. A male killer whale can be 30 feet long.

Spotted dolphins are about the size of an adult human.

The biggest dolphins are as big as a speedboat. Many species are as big as an adult human. The smallest are the size of a big dog.

Dolphins are made for swimming. Their bodies are streamlined. A streamlined body is smooth and rounded. It moves through water easily.

Dolphins move their tail up and down.

Dolphins have strong tails. A dolphin moves its tail up and down. This pushes the dolphin through the water. A dolphin also has flippers. Flippers help a dolphin steer.

This white-sided dolphin is using its flippers to balance.

You can see dolphins at a zoo. But most dolphins are wild. Dolphins live in almost every ocean in the world. Most live where the water is warm. But some live where the water is cold.

Many dolphins stay near land. They swim near the same coast, year after year. Other dolphins swim far away from land. They may travel thousands of miles.

These common dolphins are swimming near land.

Bottlenose dolphins sometimes swim into rivers.

Sometimes dolphins swim from the ocean into a river. Oceans have saltwater. Rivers have freshwater. Most ocean animals cannot live in freshwater. But some dolphins can.

Dolphins look like fish. But they are not fish. They are mammals. Mammals are animals who drink their mother's milk. People, dogs, and cats are mammals, too.

All mammals breathe air. Dolphins live in water. But they swim to the water's surface to breathe. Dolphins breathe through a blowhole. A dolphin's blowhole is an opening on the top of its head.

This is a shark. Dolphins and sharks look a bit alike. But dolphins are mammals. Sharks are fish.

All mammals have hair. Dolphins do not have much hair. Sometimes a baby dolphin has whiskers on its chin. The whiskers go away as the baby grows up.

Dolphins have a blowhole on the top of their head. They open and close their blowhole with muscles.

This gray whale is a baleen whale. You can see the baleen hanging from the whale's mouth. Inset: This is a close-up of a gray whale's baleen.

Dolphins are related to whales. There are two main groups of whales. The two groups are baleen (bah-LEEN) whales and toothed whales. Dolphins are a kind of toothed whale. Dolphins and all toothed whales have teeth. Baleen whales have baleen instead of teeth.

16

Above: *This is a pilot whale. A pilot whale is a kind of dolphin.* Below: *Like all toothed whales, dolphins have teeth.*

Chapter 2

A squid makes a good meal for a dolphin. What other animals do dolphins eat?

Fishing with Sound

Dolphins are predators (PREH-duh-turz). Predators are animals who hunt and eat other animals. The animals a predator hunts are its prey. A dolphin's prey can be ocean animals such as squid. But usually, dolphins hunt fish.

Herring, sardines, and tuna are all fish that dolphins hunt. All these kinds of fish live in schools. A school is a group of animals who swim together. Most dolphins travel in schools, too.

Dolphins eat small tuna such as these skipjack tuna.

Some dolphins hunt for prey during the day. In clear, shallow water, dolphins can see prey easily. But it is hard to see prey in deep, dark water.

Some dolphins rest during the day. They hunt at night. The water is dark at night. It is even harder to see prey.

In dark water, dolphins use echoes to tell where things are.

A dolphin can find prey even when it is hard to see. That is because a dolphin can "see" with echoes (EH-kohz). An echo is a sound that bounces off an object.

Have you ever made an echo? You can make an echo with your voice. If you shout at a wall, the sound of your voice travels to the wall. The sound may bounce back to you.

To make an echo, a dolphin makes a high sound. People cannot hear a sound this high.

But a dolphin can. The sound travels through the water. If the sound hits something, the sound bounces back to the dolphin. The dolphin hears an echo.

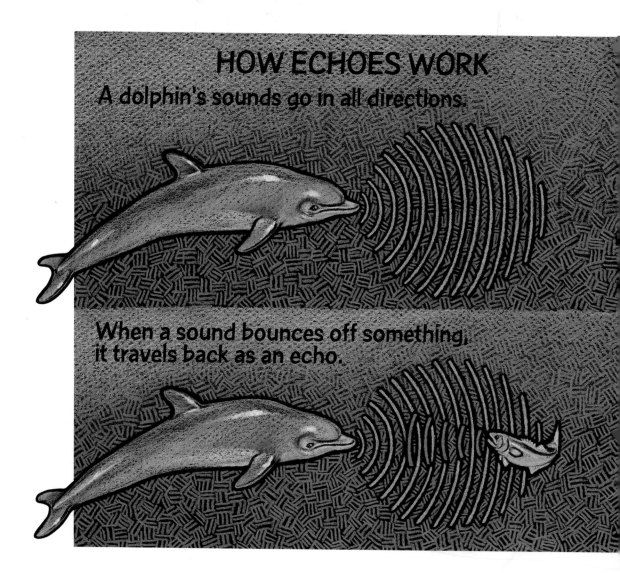

HOW ECHOES WORK

A dolphin's sounds go in all directions.

When a sound bounces off something, it travels back as an echo.

A dolphin is chasing a school of fish.

An echo tells a dolphin a lot. It tells the location of the object. Location is where something is. An echo from the left means something is on the left.

An echo also tells whether something is located near or far away. If something is near, the echo bounces back fast. If something is far away, the echo takes longer. Using echoes to know location is called echolocation (EH-koh-loh-KAY-shuhn).

Echoes help a dolphin find prey.

Echolocation also tells a dolphin what something is. That is because dolphins can tell echoes apart. The echo from a fish sounds different than the echo from a rock.

A dolphin can hear well. But it cannot hear well with its ears. A dolphin's ears are tiny slits. The slits are blocked with a plug. The plug keeps water out.

Dolphins can hear echoes from miles away.

This girl is touching a dolphin's melon. A dolphin's melon is filled with oily fat.

To hear, a dolphin uses its whole head. Its jawbone carries sound to its brain. Its melon carries sound, too. The melon is the top part of a dolphin's head. A dolphin's jawbone and melon help it hear well.

Chapter 3

Dolphins swim in schools. How many dolphins swim in one school?

Dolphin Schools

Most dolphins live in schools. The dolphins in a school stay together. They travel together. They rest together.

A school has dolphins of all ages. The youngest are newborns. The oldest may be 30 years old.

Some schools are small. Some are big.
The size depends on the species of dolphin.
A school of bottlenose dolphins may have 10 to
25 dolphins. A school of spotted dolphins may
have 1,000 dolphins.

Some dolphins stay in the same school all their life.
Some dolphins move from school to school.

A bull shark is swimming near dolphins. Bull sharks hunt dolphins.

Dolphins in a school work together. They help each other watch for predators. Sharks are predators of dolphins. Staying with the school helps keep a dolphin safe from predators.

Dolphins in a school also help each other catch fish. Sometimes they herd fish. To herd fish, dolphins swim under a school of fish. They make the fish swim to the water's surface. The dolphins stay around the fish. The fish cannot easily escape. They are easy to catch.

Dolphins in a school often follow a leader.

When a dolphin is swimming fast, it leaps to breathe.

A dolphin needs to stay with its school. Underwater, it is hard for a dolphin to see where its whole school is. Dolphins jump and splash when they swim. The dolphins underwater can hear the splashing. Then they can tell where the whole school is.

Dolphins in a school talk to each other. They whistle and click and chirp. People can hear these sounds. Each dolphin sounds different. Dolphins can tell each other apart by their voices.

No one knows for sure what dolphin sounds mean. Maybe a whistle means, "Here are some fish. Let's eat." Maybe a click means, "Be careful. I see a shark." Maybe dolphin sounds help dolphins to stay in their school.

People can hear dolphins whistle and click and chirp.

Chapter 4

A dolphin mother stays near her baby. What does a baby dolphin do when it is born?

Mothers and Babies

A baby dolphin is called a calf. Usually a mother has one calf at a time. A calf can be born at any time of year. Most calves are born in spring and summer.

A dolphin calf is born underwater. It is born near the surface. Right away, it swims to the surface. Sometimes the mother helps. She gently pushes the calf upward. The calf takes its first breath. When the calf's lungs are full of air, it swims back underwater.

A dolphin calf needs to breathe right after it is born.

A calf drinks milk from its mother. This is called nursing. All mammals nurse. A dolphin calf nurses for more than a year.

A mother and her calf talk to each other. A newborn can whistle and click. But its voice is weak. Its voice gets stronger as it gets older.

This calf is probably nursing.

A mother and her calf talk to each other.

Father dolphins live in the school with mothers and calves. But fathers do not help to raise calves. A mother raises her calf. She teaches it to hunt for food. Sometimes other females help her.

A dolphin mother does not catch fish for her calf. When a calf is about three months old, it can hunt. It catches fish for itself.

A baby dolphin is swimming with this school.

A calf stays near its mother for two or three years. Then the mother has another calf. The first calf stays in the school. It swims and hunts with the school. When a female dolphin is about 12 years old, she is old enough to have calves of her own.

Young or old, dolphins like to play. These dolphins are playing with a weed.

Chapter 5

This dolphin is swimming in front of a boat. What can people learn from dolphins?

People and Dolphins

People learn a lot by watching dolphins. We learn about how animals talk. We learn about echolocation. We learn how animals work together.

People used to hunt dolphins. But people cannot hunt dolphins anymore. Laws protect dolphins from hunting.

People sometimes hurt dolphins by dumping junk into the water. A dolphin may eat the junk. The junk can choke the dolphin. Chemicals that people put in water can make dolphins sick. Ships carry oil. Sometimes the oil spills into the water. Oil makes dolphins sick, too.

This dolphin is eating a fish that lives in sand. A dolphin might think a piece of junk is food.

Sometimes people fish in the ocean. They set fishing nets underwater. Dolphins sometimes swim into the nets. They get tangled and trapped. A dolphin has to breathe air to live. If a dolphin is trapped underwater, it dies.

A dolphin is swimming out of a fishing net. A diver is helping the dolphin.

This is a label on a can of tuna fish. The tuna was caught with nets that do not trap dolphins.

People are finding new ways to fish without hurting dolphins. Some fishermen use nets that are safe for dolphins. Dolphins can get out of these nets.

Like all wild animals, dolphins need clean places to live.

Healthy dolphins are a joy to see.

A healthy dolphin is wonderful to see. Let's make sure the world has lots of healthy dolphins. Then we can always say, "Hooray for dolphins!"

On Sharing a Book

As you know, adults greatly influence a child's attitude toward reading. When a child sees you read, or when you share a book with a child, you're sending a message that reading is important. Show the child that reading a book together is important to you. Find a comfortable, quiet place. Turn off the television and limit other distractions such as telephone calls.

Be prepared to start slowly. Take turns reading parts of this book. Stop and talk about what you're reading. Talk about the photographs. You may find that much of the shared time is spent discussing just a few pages. This discussion time is valuable for both of you, so don't move through the book too quickly. If the child begins to lose interest, stop reading. Continue sharing the book at another time. When you do pick up the book again, be sure to revisit the parts you have already read. Most importantly, enjoy the book!

Be a Vocabulary Detective

You will find a word list on page 5. Words selected for this list are important to the understanding of the topic of this book. Encourage the child to be a word detective and search for the words as you read the book together. Talk about what the words mean and how they are used in the sentence. Do any of these words have more than one meaning? You will find these words defined in a glossary on page 46.

What about Questions?

Use questions to make sure the child understands the information in this book. Here are some suggestions:

What did this paragraph tell us? What does this picture show? What do you think we'll learn about next? How many kinds of dolphins are there? Where do dolphins live? Could a dolphin live in your backyard? Why/Why not? How are dolphins like people? How are they different? What do dolphins eat? How do dolphins find their food? How long does a baby dolphin stay with its mother? What do you think it's like being a dolphin? What is your favorite part of the book? Why?

If the child has questions, don't hesitate to respond with questions of your own such as: What do *you* think? Why? What is it that you don't know? If the child can't remember certain facts, turn to the index.

Introducing the Index

The index is an important learning tool. It helps readers get information quickly without searching throughout the whole book. Turn to the index on page 47. Choose an entry such as *tail* and ask the child to use the index to find out how dolphins use their tail. Repeat this exercise with as many entries as you like. Ask the child to point out the differences between an index and a glossary. (The index helps readers find information quickly, while the glossary tells readers what words mean.)

Where in the World?

Many plants and animals found in the Early Bird Nature Books series live in parts of the world other than the United States. Encourage the child to find the places mentioned in this book on a world map or globe. Take time to talk about climate, terrain, and how you might live in such places.

All the World in Metric!

Although our monetary system is in metric units (based on multiples of 10), the United States is one of the few countries in the world that does not use the metric system of measurement. Here are some conversion activities you and the child can do using a calculator:

WHEN YOU KNOW:	MULTIPLY BY:	TO FIND:
miles	1.609	kilometers
feet	0.3048	meters
inches	2.54	centimeters
gallons	3.787	liters
pounds	0.454	kilograms

Activities

Pretend you're a dolphin. Stand in a dark place and close your eyes. Be very still and listen. How many kinds of sounds can you hear? Are the sounds near or far away? What do you think it's like to listen for echoes in ocean water?

Visit a zoo or aquarium to see dolphins, porpoises, seals, and other mammals who live in the water. How are dolphins similar to these animals? How are they different? Visit sharks at the same zoo or aquarium. How are dolphins similar to sharks? How are they different?

Glossary

blowhole—the opening on top of a dolphin's head. A dolphin breathes through its blowhole.

calf—a baby dolphin

echoes (EH-kohz)—sounds that bounce off objects

echolocation (EH-koh-loh-KAY-shuhn)—using echoes to know where things are

mammals—animals who drink their mother's milk, breathe air, and have hair

melon—the part of a dolphin's head that helps it to hear

nursing—drinking mother's milk

predators (PREH-duh-turz)—animals who hunt and eat other animals

prey—animals who are hunted and eaten by other animals

schools—groups of animals who swim together

streamlined—smooth and rounded

Index

About the Author

Leighton Taylor is a marine biologist who began studying the sea while fishing as a small boy in California. He went to graduate school in Hawaii. Hawaii's warm water, bright fish, and coral reefs convinced him to spend his life studying and writing about the animals who live in the sea. He earned a Ph.D. degree at Scripps Institution of Oceanography. He loves to dive and has made many expeditions in the Pacific Ocean, the Indian Ocean, and the Caribbean Sea. He has discovered and named several new species of sharks, including the deep-sea Megamouth shark.

About the Photographer

Norbert Wu's photography has appeared in numerous books, films, and magazines—including *Audubon, Harper's, International Wildlife, Le Figaro, National Geographic, Omni, Outside,* and *Smithsonian*—and on the covers of *GEO, Natural History, Time,* and *Terre Sauvage.* The author and photographer of several books on wildlife and photography, his photographic library of marine and topside wildlife is one of the most comprehensive in the world. His recent projects include television filming for National Geographic Television, Survival Anglia, and PBS.

The Early Bird Nature Books Series

African Elephants
Alligators
Ants
Apple Trees
Bobcats
Brown Bears
Cats
Cockroaches
Cougars
Crayfish
Dandelions
Dolphins
Giant Sequoia Trees
Herons

Horses
Jellyfish
Manatees
Moose
Mountain Goats
Mountain Gorillas
Peacocks
Penguins
Polar Bears
Popcorn Plants
Prairie Dogs
Rats
Red-Eyed Tree Frogs
Saguaro Cactus

Sandhill Cranes
Scorpions
Sea Lions
Sea Turtles
Slugs
Swans
Tarantulas
Tigers
Venus Flytraps
Vultures
Walruses
Whales
White-Tailed Deer
Wild Turkeys